General Introduction

Unbound Project

In the 41 years between the publication of the first and the last of McLuhan's writings represented here, his thinking, like the river Liffey in *Finnegans Wake*, enriched itself from all that it touched and returned to its starting point. His intellectual odyssey during those four decades took him from the study of English literature (see "G. K. Chesterton: A Practical Mystic") to a ground-breaking fusion of philosophy, psychology, sociology, and anthropology (see "Laws of Media"). In between, he called for a program of educational reform, dictated by the dominance of electric technology. But this program, based on the analysis of media, was already implicit in techniques of language control that McLuhan had assimilated in his days as a graduate student in the Cambridge University English School.

It was his genius to refine and expand those techniques, to put them in a larger context, to apply them to the whole of human experience and social organization by defining a medium as any extension of body or mind. With this single stroke, McLuhan effectively scrapped the distinctions between words and things, set words and weapons on the same footing as the telephone and television, or money and movies, developed a unified and integrated framework of analysis to allow himself and his readers to get "Inside Blake and Hollywood" (q.v.).

The present collection of twenty pieces from McLuhan's pen, never previously assembled, affords a unique and rich glimpse of both the variety of his interests and the unity of his thought. Here is McLuhan's literary analysis, indelibly stamped with the influence of Practical Criticism, absorbed from I. A. Richards, F. R. Leavis, and other Cambridge luminaries under whom he studied in the 1930s. Here is his take on the world of advertising ("American Advertising") published before his first book on the same theme (*The Mechanical Bride*, first edition, 1951; Gingko Press, 2002) and providing a counterpoint to the latter. Here are the first fruits of the interdisciplinary seminars he conducted with colleagues at the University of Toronto in the 1950 s.

Already, at that time, the themes that would be fully developed in his *Understanding Media* (first edition, 1964; Gingko Press, 2003) begin to appear in his contributions to the journal *Explorations*, the outgrowth of those seminars. (See "Culture Without Literacy," "New Media as Political Forms," "New Media as Art Forms," "Media Fit the Battle of Jericho.") The gestation of *The Gutenberg Galaxy* (1962) emerges from the same texts, and from others such as "Printing and Social Change" and "The Effect of the Printed Book on Language in the Sixteenth Century." Published originally within the five years preceding the appearance of *The Gutenberg Galaxy*, these two texts not only point toward the book but continue to stand as valuable adjuncts to it.

The former clarifies the distinction between participation as a mental activity and participation as the degree of involvement of the organs of perception, comments on the analysis of process and movement as the matrix of both production and consumption of print, notes the inverse correlation between linguistic complexity and the cultural effects of technology on language, and explicitly refuses relativism (opting instead for the investigation of the psychodynamics of technological change). The latter offers a concise lesson on the limits of metaphor through commentary on the dynamics of acoustic space, counter-intuitive observations (photography tends toward the auditory), an outline of the correlation between the complexity of language structure and sensory bias, and a graphic snapshot of the semiotic reduction precipitated by print technology.

Semiotics was the framework within which Ferdinand de Saussure set his pioneering approach to linguistics at the beginning of the twentieth century. McLuhan came to Saussure late in his career, but passages from various texts in *McLuhan Unbound* such as "At the Moment of Sputnik" and "Myth and Mass Media" suggest the common ground between some of the most fundamental notions in the thought of Saussure and McLuhan. At the same time, it is pertinent to note McLuhan's explicit distinction between the structuralism that has its roots in symbolist poetry and painting and the structures implicit in linguistics as practiced at the midpoint of the twentieth century. In "The Medium is the Message," he explains how the structural linguist could be wrong.

The texts gathered here consistently complement each other: "New Media as Art Forms" and "New Media as Political Forms;" "The Argument: Causality in the Electric World" and "The Relation of Environment to Anti-Environment." Read for their complementarities, they yield insights into the method and the meaning, the medium and the message, the percepts and the program of Marshall McLuhan, the media analyst and educational reformer.

W. Terrence Gordon

Marshall McLuhan Unbound Project Editors
Eric McLuhan, W. Terrence Gordon

Gingko Press, Inc.
5768 Paradise Drive, Suite J • Corte Madera, CA 94925
(415) 924-9615 • Fax (415) 924-9608
email: books@gingkopress.com
http://www.gingkopress.com

ISBN: 1-58423-051-7

Selected by Eric McLuhan
General introduction and essay introductions © 2005 W. Terrence Gordon
With very special thanks to Eric McLuhan, Corinne McLuhan and Matie Molinaro
Libray of Congress Control Number 2005927213

Design, packaging and production: Die Gestalten Verlag, Berlin
Layout and Typography: onlab, Berlin
Fonts: *Dolly* by Underware, *Bullet* by House Industries
Production: Martin Bretschneider, Vinzenz Geppert
Art direction: Robert Klanten

Made in Germany